W9-ABY-470

Folktales and Legends

Written by Denise Bieniek
Illustrated by Laura Ferraro

Troll Associates

NO LONGER THE PROPERTY
OF THE
UNIVERSITY OF R. I. LIBRARY

Metric Conversion Chart

1 inch = 2.54 centimeters	1 fluid ounce (oz.) = 29.573 milliliters
1 foot = .305 meter	1 cup = .24 liter
1 yard = .914 meter	1 pint = .473 liter
1 mile = 1.61 kilometers	1 teaspoon = 4.93 milliliters

Copyright © 1996 by Troll Communications L.L.C. Published by Troll Associates, an imprint and registered trademark of Troll Communications L.L.C. All rights reserved. Permission is hereby granted to the purchaser to reproduce these pages, in sufficient quantities to meet yearly student needs, for use in the buyer's classroom. All other permissions must be obtained from the publisher.

Printed in the United States of America.
10 9 8 7 6 5 4 3 2

Contents

Why Dogs and Cats Don't Get Along 5–6

Dogs and Cats Flannel Board 7–9

Dogs and Cats Matching Activity 10

Rice Barrel Measurements 11

Dog and Cat Word Search 12

Don't Let the Dog In! 13

The Flip Side Class Book 14–15

The Proud Goanna Puppet Theater 16–21

Proud Goanna Questions 22

Classmate Comparisons 23

Goanna Colors 24

Compare/Contrast 25

The Peculiar Such Thing 26–27

The Peculiar Such Thing Display 28

Goosebumps Scramble 29

"It Happened Like This . . ." Bulletin Board 30–31

Spooky Sizes Activity Poster 32–33

Johnny Appleseed File-Folder Game 34–37

Little Red Riding Hood 38–39

Little Red Riding Hood Flannel Board 40–42

Through the Woods 43

Little Red Adjectives 44

Wolf Paper-Bag Costume 45

Wolf Mask 46

Paul Bunyan and His Blue Ox 47–48

Paul Bunyan and Babe Stick Puppets 49–51

Where in the World? 52

Missing Words 53

The Sorcerer's Apprentice Rebus Story 54–55

The Sorcerer's Apprentice Paper-Bag Puppets 56–59

Magical Opposites 60

First Things First 61

Awards 62-63

Answers 64

Why Dogs and Cats Don't Get Along

A Korean folktale

Once, a long time ago, a man named Shu lived in a village by a river with his dog and his cat. The dog and cat were the best of friends, and the three lived quite happily in their little house.

To make his living, Shu sold rice to the villagers. Everyone in the village came to buy their rice from Shu. No matter how many people came, he always had enough rice to sell them. The villagers wondered how Shu got so much rice, but they never asked him—and he never told them.

Shu had not always had a full barrel of rice. At one time he was quite poor. But one day, when Shu was down to his last bowl of rice, a traveling monk came to his house and asked, "Sir, could you spare a bowl of rice for a man who has traveled great distances?"

Shu thought, "This man must be very hungry indeed. I will share what I have with him." So Shu gave his last bowl of rice to the monk.

When the monk had finished, he said, "Kind sir, here is a magic coin in return for your generosity. Put this coin in a barrel with a few grains of rice and you will never want for rice again." As soon as the monk left, Shu ran to a neighbor's house and asked to borrow some rice. He placed it, along with the magic coin, in a barrel. Bursting with excitement, Shu opened the lid just a little. The barrel was filled to the brim with rice. Shu took a bowlful to his neighbor to repay him. When he returned, the barrel was full again. And so Shu opened his rice store after that and made a good living.

One day, when Shu went to get some rice, there were only a few grains left at the bottom of the barrel. Shu looked for his magic coin, but it was not to be found. "Oh, no!" he said. "I must have scooped it up with the last rice that was bought. We must find it! Oh, what will happen to me?"

Shu looked everywhere in the house for the coin, but it was not there. The dog and the cat, who knew Shu's secret, decided to help him look for the coin. They searched the whole town, but it was nowhere to be found. Next, the dog and cat decided to look across the river. Since it was winter, the river was frozen, and they quickly walked across its icy surface.

© 1996 Troll Associates/ Troll Early Learning Activities *Folktales and Legends*

Why Dogs and Cats Don't Get Along

After weeks of looking, they located the coin in a house filled with rats. It was locked inside a chest, and the dog and cat had no way of getting it out. They decided to make a deal with the rats. "We will not bother you for ten years if you gnaw a hole in the chest and give us our coin," the dog and cat offered. The rats agreed, and soon the coin was out of the chest.

When the dog and cat got back to the river, they saw that it had thawed over the spring. The cat wailed, "I cannot swim. How will I get back to our house?" The dog replied, "Climb on my back, and I will carry you across."

So the cat put the coin in his mouth and climbed on the dog's back. The dog started the swim across the river. The children swimming in the river and those playing by its edge began pointing and laughing at the pair. They had never seen such a sight! The dog swam on, stony-faced. The cat, however, realized what a silly pair they made, and he began to laugh.

As soon as he opened his mouth, the coin dropped out and drifted to the bottom of the river. The dog could not believe his eyes. "You fool!" he shouted angrily. The dog was so furious that he shook the cat off his back and swam to shore.

The cat barely made it to the shore. When he reached land, the dog tried to attack him. To get away, the terrified cat ran up a tree. He coughed and spit out the water he had swallowed from the river.

And that is why, today, dogs try to bite cats, and cats hiss and spit at dogs.

And what ever became of poor Shu? Well, his dog waited at the river's edge trying to figure out how he could get the coin from the bottom of the river. One day the dog watched as a fisherman reeled in a large fish. He watched him cut the fish open, and saw the magic coin fall to the ground. Quickly, the dog grabbed the coin and ran home to Shu. The dog and Shu lived happily ever after, selling rice in their village by the river.

Discussion Questions:

1. Have you ever seen a dog and a cat together? What happened?
2. Describe what life might be like living near a river.
3. Describe the friendship between the three main characters.
4. What do you think Shu did while the dog and cat were away searching for the coin?
5. Do you think the dog and the cat kept their promise not to bother the rats for ten years?
6. Name three adjectives for each period in Shu's life: as a poor man; as a rich man; when he lost his coin; and when he got it back.
7. What do you think happened to the cat?
8. Find Korea on a world map. How might you travel there?

© 1996 Troll Associates/ Troll Early Learning Activities

Dogs and Cats Flannel Board

Materials:

- crayons or markers
- scissors
- medium-weight interfacing or flannel scraps
- glue
- plastic bag

Directions:

1. Reproduce the patterns on pages 7–9. Ask students to color the shapes and cut them out.

2. Glue medium-weight interfacing or flannel scraps to the back of each figure and object.

3. Display the figures and shapes to the class. Before reading the story, ask students to identify them and tell what, if anything, they know about them. For example, you may wish to hold up the rice barrel and ask students if they have ever eaten rice. Have them describe how it looks before and after it is cooked. Ask volunteers to explain how their families cook rice. Teach the class some ways of saying rice in different languages. Ask who likes rice and who does not.

4. While you read the story, place the appropriate character or object on the flannel board. Or let students add the pieces to the board themselves.

5. Leave the pieces in a plastic bag hanging near the flannel board so students may retell the story and use the pieces during free time.

© 1996 Troll Associates/ Troll Early Learning Activities

Folktales and Legends

Dogs and Cats Flannel Board

© 1996 Troll Associates/ Troll Early Learning Activities

Folktales and Legends

© 1996 Troll Associates/ Troll Early Learning Activities

Dogs and Cats Matching Activity

Materials:

- crayons or markers
- scissors
- two large sheets of oaktag
- glue
- clear contact paper
- pocket folder

Directions:

1. Reproduce the dog and cat patterns on pages 7 and 9 twelve times each. To make patterns for a matching activity, color each of six pairs of dogs the same way, and repeat for the cat patterns. Some suggested patterns: red with orange dots, purple and yellow stripes, pink with green zigzag lines, and white with black squares. To make the activity more challenging, color two pairs of dogs or cats with similar patterns. For example, you may wish to color two cats with thin pink stripes and red stripes and two cats with wide pink stripes and red stripes.

2. Glue the dogs onto a large sheet of oaktag. Repeat the process with the cats. Cut them out again and then laminate them with clear contact paper.

3. Show the class how to use the activity. Hold up a dog and ask the class to describe its pattern. Then hold up another dog with a different pattern on it. Ask the class to tell whether it is the same or different. Continue with different dog shapes until you hold up the one that matches. When the students guess it is the same, place the pair aside. Continue with the rest of the dogs and cats.

4. Place the dogs in one pocket of a pocket folder and the cats in the other pocket. Put the folder on the bookshelf for students to use during reading time or free time.

© 1996 Troll Associates/ Troll Early Learning Activities

Folktales and Legends

Rice Barrel Measurements

Materials:

- three large sheets of brown oaktag
- scissors
- transparent tape
- 2 pounds of uncooked rice
- plastic or aluminum trays
- plastic measuring cups

Directions:

1. Inform students that they will be making rice barrels like the one in the folktale "Why Dogs and Cats Don't Get Along." Cut apart three large sheets of brown oaktag into squares ranging in size from 4" to 6" on a side. Distribute a square of oaktag to each student, along with a pair of scissors.

2. Ask each student to make a rice barrel using his or her oaktag square. Students may change the sizes of their barrels by cutting an inch or two off one or two sides. When they have decided on the size of their barrels, students should overlap the ends and tape them closed.

3. Place plastic or aluminum trays around the room. Pour some rice into a measuring cup and place it next to each tray. Ask each child to pair up with a classmate and predict which of their barrels will hold the most rice. The students in each pair should go to a tray and read the measurement on the measuring cup together. One student should then press his or her barrel firmly against the bottom of the tray. He or she can then pour the rice from the measuring cup into the barrel.

4. When the barrel is filled to the brim, have the student check the new rice measurement on the cup and subtract to figure out how much rice the barrel holds. The other partner then does the procedure with his or her barrel.

5. After the pouring and measuring is finished, ask students whether their predictions were correct. Encourage students to test their barrels with at least three other students. Then leave the barrels, the rice, and the trays in the math center for students to use during free time.

© 1996 Troll Associates/ Troll Early Learning Activities

Name _____

Dog and Cat Word Search

Find the words listed in the box below hidden in the letter jumble. Words may appear diagonally, backward, forward, or vertically.

```
O B R D C A T B I R D D R S O P A N T A C
G E E N A R E M E T A C Q A E T S A E F R
F S H A E C T U H T O O T G O D O R U P E
A T C P H P A D D O G F I S H E R A G D S
C A T A P U L T H O U S E S L L D M E O U
C T A C O B S Y A D G O D Y U S N A I G O
D O C O R K G Y J C A T A L O G A T F H H
E G G U T D O O W G O D O C D O P A R O D
R D O T S D O G G O O M E A N D K C O U D
A N D O A K R G O G O L B T A R A O E S A
E E F H T R D O G T A G I A M T C M D E P
G I H E A O F S C O L L A C T A C B O R L
O R R T C P O D A G N C A T S U P Y F M A
```

catacomb	**catbird**	**catalog**	**catamaran**
catapult	**catastrophe**	**catcall**	**catnap**
dog days	**dogwood**	**dog sled**	**dog tag**
dogcatcher	**dog paddle**	**doghouse**	**dogtooth**
catfish	**catsup**	**dog-eared**	**dogfish**

BONUS: Look up the definitions for any of the words you don't know. Write the definitions on the back of this worksheet.

© 1996 Troll Associates/ Troll Early Learning Activities

Don't Let the Dog In!

1. Have the class gather in a circle. Choose a student to be the "dog" and another to be the "cat." Ask the dog to stand outside the circle and the cat to stand inside.

2. Inform the students forming the circle that they are the walls of the house. They must try to keep the dog from getting in the house and catching the cat.

3. On the word "Go," the dog will try to find holes in the walls of the house and make his or her way in to it. The cat will try to keep as far away from the dog as possible. To "catch" the cat, the dog must tag the cat with both hands at the same time.

4. The students making up the walls may move as close together as they can to prevent the dog from getting in the house. Caution the students that they must be careful of their classmates while playing. Tell the students they must rely on quickness rather than force.

5. If the dog gets into the house, the cat may not leave the house until the other students have counted to fifteen. They may then move aside to let the cat out of the house while trying to keep the dog in. If the cat can get back in the house after the dog has left it, the round is over. A new dog and cat are chosen.

6. Continue playing for as long as interest lasts.

© 1996 Troll Associates/ Troll Early Learning Activities

The Flip Side Class Book

Materials:

- oaktag
- crayons or markers
- scissors
- glue
- 9" x 12" white construction paper
- hole puncher
- yarn

Directions:

1. Reproduce the magic coin on page 15 twice. Color the coins and cut them out. Glue the colored coins to oaktag and cut them out again. Distribute a sheet of white construction paper to each student.

2. Ask students to use the coin shapes as patterns and trace around them once on the construction paper.

3. Inform students that they will be making antonym pictures. Ask students to think up pairs of opposites. On one side of their coins, have the students draw pictures of one of their opposites. On the other side, they should draw pictures of the other opposite of their pair.

4. Have students label the pictures. Older students may write out more than one word on each side.

5. Collect all the coin pages. Punch two holes on the left side of each one, including the magic coin patterns, which will be the covers. Tie them together with 4" lengths of yarn.

6. Give the book a title and share it with the class. Ask students to read a page and then guess what the flip side of the page will say. For example, if the front page has a picture of a large dog, the students might guess that a small dog would be on the other side of the page.

7. Leave the book on the bookshelf for students to use during free time.

© 1996 Troll Associates/ Troll Early Learning Activities

Folktales and Legends

The Flip Side Class Book

BIG

TALL short

little

Hot

cold

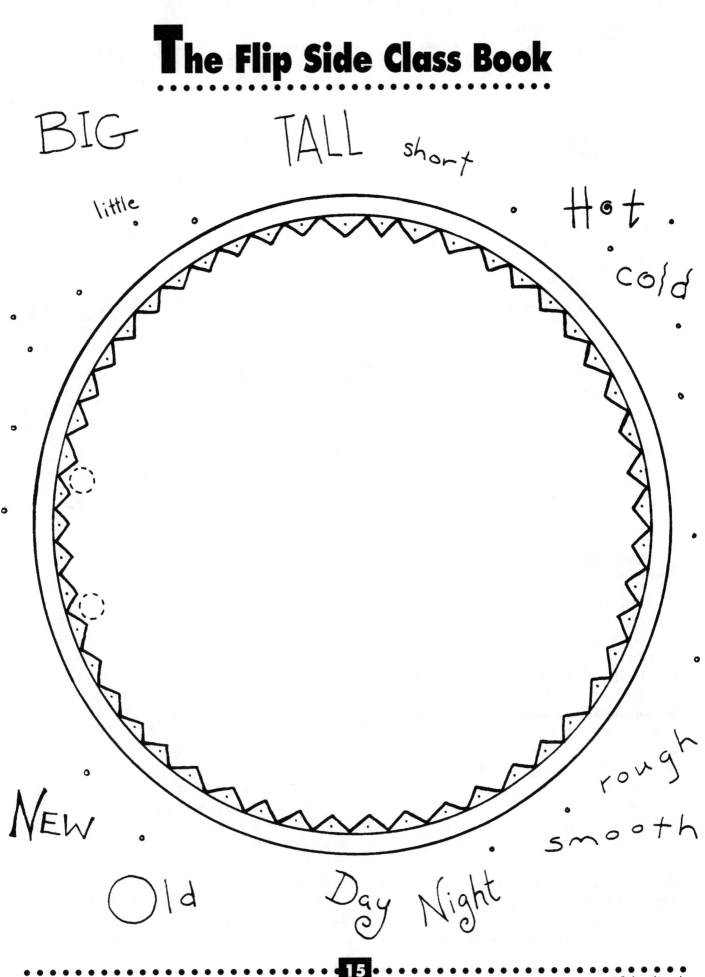

NEW

rough

smooth

Old

Day Night

© 1996 Troll Associates/ Troll Early Learning Activities

Folktales and Legends

The Proud Goanna Puppet Theater

An Australian folktale

Materials:

- scissors
- oaktag
- glue
- five yardsticks
- masking tape
- twin-sized white sheet
- strong string
- filmstrip projector or other wide-beam light

Directions:

1. Read to the class the story "The Proud Goanna," from the book *The Flying Emu* by Sally Morgan (published by Knopf, 1992). Then reproduce the story characters on pages 17–21 once. Ask students to cut them out. Mount the patterns on oaktag and cut them out again.

2. Tape a yardstick perpendicularly to the center back of each character.

3. Decide on a location in the classroom for the shadow theater. Measure the width of the stage area carefully; it should be at least the length of a twin-sized sheet.

4. Place a twin-sized white sheet on the floor. Gather one corner at the top right side and tie it with strong string.

5. Cut the string to a length corresponding to the width of the stage area. Repeat for the corner on the top left side.

6. The sheet may be hung in several ways. Two nails may be driven into opposite walls and the sheet hung between them, with the string on the two corners tied to the two nails. Or two chairs may be placed at a distance apart equal to the length of the sheet and the sheet hung between the two chairs. The string may then be tied to the chair backs, leaving some of the sheet to lay on the floor. Keep the sheet as taut as possible.

7. Position a filmstrip projector or other wide-beam light "backstage," directing the light toward the sheet. When the characters are held flat against the sheet by the end of the yardsticks, the audience sitting on the opposite side of the sheet will be able to see their silhouettes.

8. Choose five students to handle the five puppets in the show and one student to be the narrator. As the narrator reads, the puppeteers should manipulate their puppets onto and off the screen.

© 1996 Troll Associates/ Troll Early Learning Activities

Folktales and Legends

© 1996 Troll Associates/ Troll Early Learning Activities

Folktales and Legends

The Proud Goanna Puppet Theater

© 1996 Troll Associates/ Troll Early Learning Activities

The Proud Goanna Puppet Theater

© 1996 Troll Associates/ Troll Early Learning Activities

Folktales and Legends

The Proud Goanna Puppet Theater

© 1996 Troll Associates/ Troll Early Learning Activities

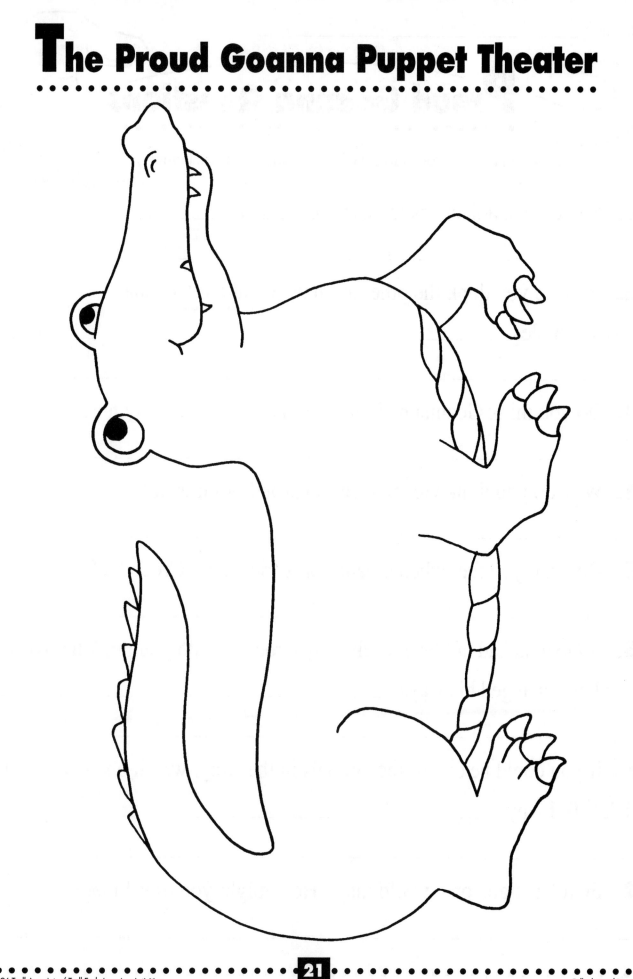

© 1996 Troll Associates/ Troll Early Learning Activities

Folktales and Legends

Name _____

Proud Goanna Questions

After hearing the story "The Proud Goanna," answer the questions below.

1. Name three adjectives to describe Goanna. _____

_____

2. How do you think the other animals felt about Goanna?

Give examples. _____

_____

3. Do you think Goanna had many friends? Why or why not?

_____

4. Why do you think Goanna was so proud of himself? _____

_____

5. How did you feel when Goanna was tricked by Crocodile?

_____

6. If Goanna had not been tricked by Crocodile, do you think he would

ever have changed his ways? _____

_____

7. If you could be one of the animals in the story, which one would you

pick? Tell why. _____

_____

8. Find Australia on a world map. How might you travel there?

_____

© 1996 Troll Associates/ Troll Early Learning Activities   Folktales and Legends

Name _____

Classmate Comparisons

In the story "The Proud Goanna," Goanna makes many comparisons between himself and the other animals in the bush. Of course, Goanna always thinks he is the best!

Comparisons show us differences and similarities. Answer the questions below about you and your classmates. Then compare your answers with your classmates'.

1. Who travels the longest distance to get to school?

_____

2. Who is the oldest person in the class? The youngest?

_____

3. Who speaks a language other than English? What language or languages? _____

4. Who has the longest hair in the class? The shortest?

_____

5. Who has the same hobbies as you? Who has a hobby with which you are not familiar? _____

6. What kinds of music do you like? _____

7. What is your favorite subject in school? _____

8. What kinds of books do you like to read? _____

_____

9. What kinds of jobs do you do at home? _____

_____

10. What makes you happy? _____

What makes you sad? _____

© 1996 Troll Associates/ Troll Early Learning Activities

Folktales and Legends

Name _____

Goanna Colors

Color all the equations that equal 7 blue.
Color all the equations that equal 8 yellow.
Color all the equations that equal 9 red.
Color all the equations that equal 10 orange.

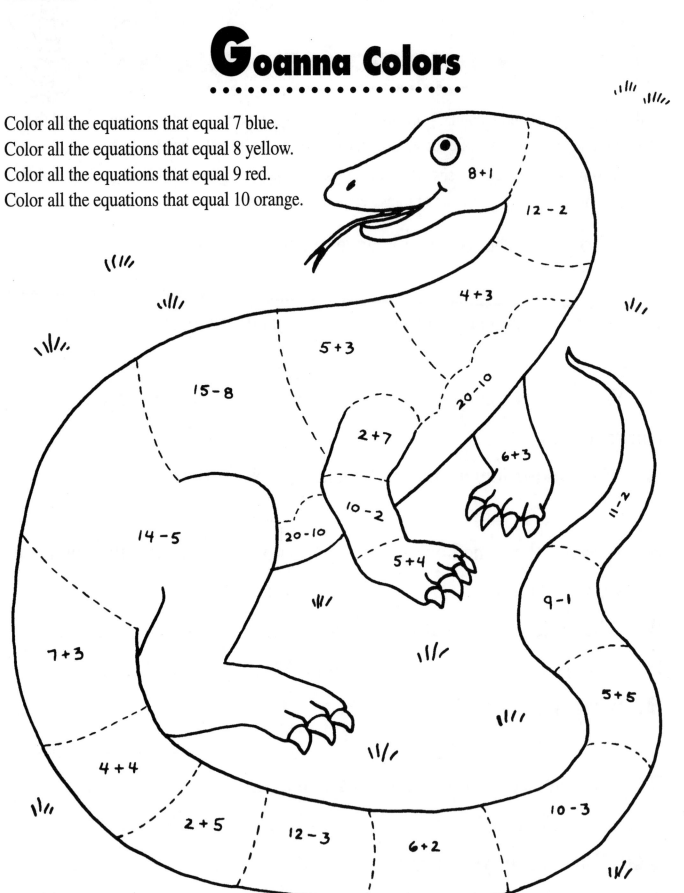

© 1996 Troll Associates/ Troll Early Learning Activities

Name _____

Compare/Contrast

Read the following fable about a proud king and what happens to him because of his pride. Then compare this story to "The Proud Goanna" and "The Tortoise and the Hare." On the back of this piece of paper, draw a Venn diagram to compare and contrast the three stories.

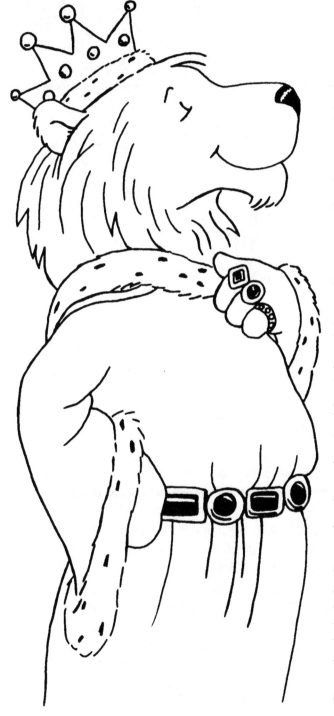

King Lion looked in the mirror and liked what he saw. He was wearing luxurious robes, a gold crown, and many rings on his fingers. He decided to go out and show himself to his subjects.

As he walked, he made sure that everyone who saw him bowed to the ground. As he approached a small beetle, he asked, "Why aren't you bowing to me, Beetle?" The beetle replied that he was; the king only had to bend down to see him. The king bent over but still could not see the tiny beetle. The beetle asked him to bend a little lower. When the king did so, his crown rolled off his head, his robes fell from his shoulders, and he lost his balance. The king ended up in a ditch by the side of the road, covered with mud.

© 1996 Troll Associates/ Troll Early Learning Activities   Folktales and Legends

The Peculiar Such Thing

An African folktale

Deep in the woods, a man lived all alone in a small log cabin. There was an old fireplace on one wall where he cooked his supper. One night, after the man had eaten his supper, something crept through a crack between the logs. It was the most peculiar such thing the man had ever seen.

And this peculiar such thing had a great, big, long tail. When the man saw this something with the great, big, long tail, he grabbed his axe and chopped the tail right off the peculiar such thing. And you know what that man did with that great, big, long tail? He ate it. And after eating his whole supper, too!

Later that night, when the man was in bed, he heard something climbing up the side of his log cabin. He heard it scratching. And then he heard it say, "Tailypo, tailypo, give me my tailypo." The man called to his dogs, who were lying in the space beneath the cabin. "Perfect!" (because the first dog did everything right). "Tolerable and OK!" (because they were just average). "Go see!" And those dogs came out from under the house lickety split. The dogs chased the peculiar such thing far away. And so the man went to sleep.

In the middle of the next night, the man heard something at the front door trying to get in. It was trying to tear the door down. He heard it say, "Tailypo, tailypo, I want my tailypo." The man called his dogs from under the house. They chased that peculiar such thing far away again. And so the man went to sleep.

It was still a long way until morning when the man woke up because he heard something down by the swamp. It said, "I know you have it. I want it. Give me my tailypo!" The man called his dogs again, "Perfect! Tolerable! OK!" But the dogs didn't come. It must have been that the peculiar such thing had eaten them up.

© 1996 Troll Associates/ Troll Early Learning Activities

Folktales and Legends

The man was scared, but he fell asleep anyway. At daybreak, the man heard scratching. He heard tearing. He looked down at the foot of his bed. He saw two pointy little ears coming over the edge of the bed. In a minute, he saw two beady little red eyes. The man was so scared he couldn't scream. He couldn't move.

The peculiar such thing kept crawling up the bed. Closer and closer it came, scratching and tearing as it got even closer to the man. Soon it was sitting on the man's chest. It screamed, "Tailypo, tailypo, give me my tailypo!" The man told him, "I don't have it. I don't have it."

The peculiar such thing screamed back, "Yes, you have it! And I'm going to get it back!" And so it did.

Folks who live around the man's log cabin say that when the wind is blowing, they can hear some peculiar such thing calling " . . . tailypo . . . tailypo. . . ." And then the sound fades away like it never was.

Discussion Questions:

1. Where do you think the peculiar such thing lives? How do you think it came into being?

2. If you were the man, what would you have done when the peculiar such thing came into your log cabin?

3. How do you think the man felt every time he heard the peculiar such thing clawing to get to him?

4. Do you think the end of the story was scary?

5. How do you think the people who live near the man's log cabin feel when they hear the wind blowing "tailypo . . . tailypo . . ."?

6. Can you think of a new ending to the story?

The Peculiar Such Thing Display

Materials:

- crayons or markers
- construction paper
- paper towel tubes
- brown paper lunch bags
- collage materials
- clean junk
- dry beans, pebbles, rice

- scissors
- glue
- paints and paintbrushes

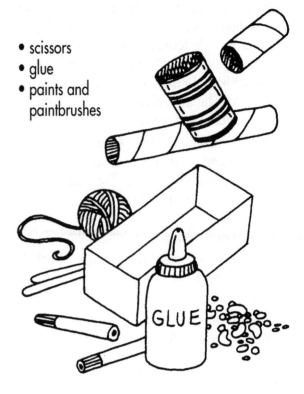

Directions:

1. Brainstorm with the class about what the peculiar such thing might look like. Write down all the students' comments on the chalkboard. Then ask them to categorize their comments under any appropriate headings they can make up.

2. Inform the class that they will be making models of the peculiar such things. Give them a few minutes to decide what their creatures will look like. Tell the students that there are only two rules they must follow: the creature must have a moving part, and it must make some sort of noise.

3. Distribute crayons or markers and construction paper and have students sketch what their peculiar such things will look like. After getting their rough sketches down, they may begin making foundations for their creatures, using paper towel tubes, lunch bags, or clean junk (such as shoe boxes or scraps of wood).

4. When the basic body is finished, students may decorate their creations with collage materials, construction paper, other decorative paper, or paint. Remind students of the two rules for making their creatures.

5. Students may wish to use dry beans, pebbles, or rice to help their creatures make noise.

6. Ask each student to come before the class with their peculiar such thing. Have them demonstrate how it moves and how it makes its noise. Ask students if they have any comments about their classmates' work.

7. Display the creations around the room or grouped on one shelf with the title "Our Peculiar Such Things."

© 1996 Troll Associates/ Troll Early Learning Activities

Name _____

Goosebumps Scramble

Unscramble the words below. Write the unscrambled words on the lines provided.

1. orltl _____

2. stogh _____

3. holug _____

4. tronsem _____

5. preamiv _____

6. flowerew _____

7. boling _____

8. chiwt _____

9. lemgrin _____

10. thonmap _____

11. tigan _____

12. rloawkc _____

© 1996 Troll Associates/ Troll Early Learning Activities

Foltales and Legends

"It Happened Like This . . ." Bulletin Board

Materials:

- crayons or markers
- scissors
- dark blue bulletin board paper
- stapler
- 9" x 12" white construction paper

Directions:

1. Reproduce the patterns on page 31 twenty times. Ask students to color the patterns and cut them out.

2. Cover a bulletin board with dark blue paper. Staple the spooky creatures around the edges of the board as a border.

3. Cut a large circle from a sheet of 9" x 12" white construction paper and staple it to the board at the top center; this will be the full moon.

4. Ask the class to divide up into pairs. Ask the pairs to choose a scary story they have read or heard, or to use "The Peculiar Such Thing." The pairs will recreate the stories they have chosen from the viewpoints of each story's "monster." For example, a pair of students might choose to use the story "The Big Toe," in which an old woman out on a walk finds a toe and brings it home. Eventually, something finds its way into her house and comes

closer and closer and says louder and louder, "Give me back my big toe!" Students can tell the story from the viewpoint of the creature that comes looking for its big toe, beginning by telling how the something lost its toe, how it was looking for it when some stranger came by and picked it up, and how it felt when that happened. They could then go on to describe how it didn't mean to scare the old lady but was so eager to get its toe back that the words just came out too loudly. Remind students that stories may be told comically or dramatically.

5. When the partners are finished writing their monster-viewpoint story, have them draw scenes from their story on 9" x 12" white construction paper. Staple the drawings onto the bulletin board under the title "It Happened Like This . . ."

6. Invite students to read each other's work and make comments.

© 1996 Troll Associates/ Troll Early Learning Activities

Folktales and Legends

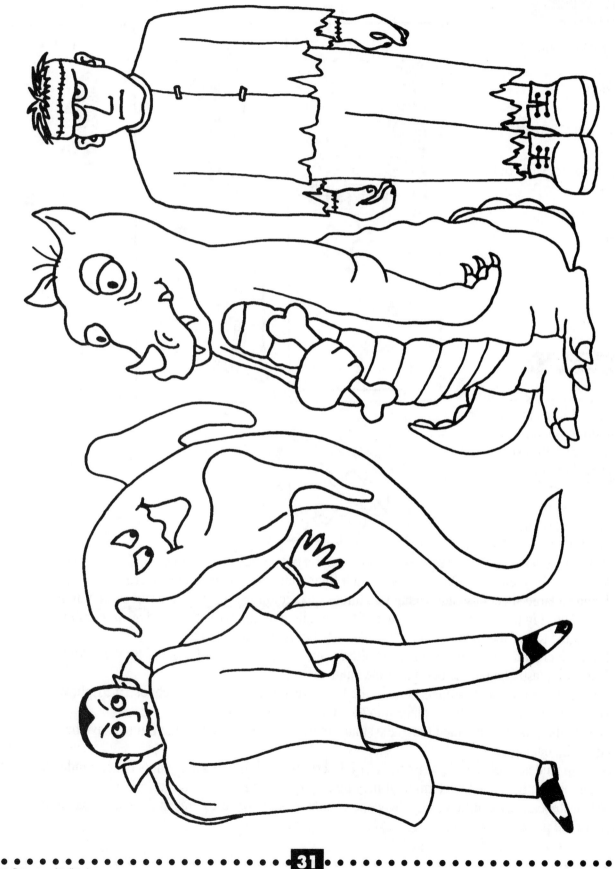

© 1996 Troll Associates/ Troll Early Learning Activities

"It Happened Like This . . ." Bulletin Board

Spooky Sizes Activity Poster

Directions:

- crayons or markers
- scissors
- oaktag
- glue
- clear contact paper
- Velcro
- large sheet of white oaktag
- ruler
- clear plastic bag
- stapler

Materials:

1. Reproduce the creatures on page 33 three times. For the first reproduction, set the machine for 100% size. For the second reproduction, set the machine at 75% (for a 25% reduction). For the last reproduction, set the machine at 50% (for a 50% reduction).

2. Ask students to color the creatures, mount them on oaktag, and cut them out.

3. Laminate the creatures. On the back of each figure, attach a piece of soft Velcro.

4. Divide a large sheet of white oaktag into three equal columns. At the top of the left column, write the word *big* in big letters. At the top of the middle column, write the word *medium* in medium letters. At the top of the right column, write the word *little* in little letters.

5. For each creature to be placed in each column, attach a piece of hard Velcro into the column. Staple a clear plastic bag to the bottom of the oaktag sheet.

6. To play the game, show students one of the large creatures. Ask them to choose the right word to describe its size. Ask a student to place it in the appropriate column.

7. Repeat the process for a medium and a small figure. Continue until all the figures have been placed on the oaktag chart.

8. To help students self-check, write the word describing each figure's size on its back. Students may then look on the back to determine if they placed the creature in the correct column.

9. When students are finished using the game, they may store the creatures in the plastic bag at the bottom of the poster.

© 1996 Troll Associates/ Troll Early Learning Activities

Spooky Sizes Activity Poster

© 1996 Troll Associates/ Troll Early Learning Activities

Folktales and Legends

Johnny Appleseed File-Folder Game

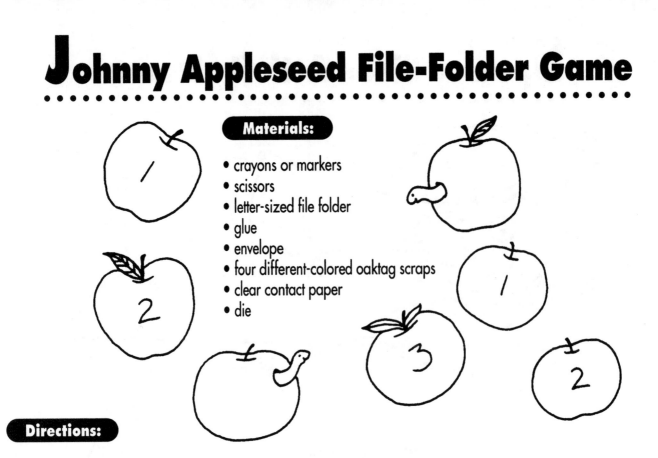

Materials:

- crayons or markers
- scissors
- letter-sized file folder
- glue
- envelope
- four different-colored oaktag scraps
- clear contact paper
- die

Directions:

1. Reproduce the game board on pages 35 and 36. Color the game board and cut it out.
2. Glue the game board to the inside of a letter-sized file folder. Reproduce the "How to Play" instructions and glue them to the front of the file folder.
3. Reproduce the apple game pieces on page 37 four times. Color the apples, mount them on oaktag, and cut them out. Laminate the apples.
4. To make the playing pieces, cut 1" squares from four different colors of oaktag scraps.
5. Glue an envelope to the back of the file folder. Store the apples, playing pieces, and the die in the envelope.

How to Play (for 2–4 players)
1. Give each player four apple game pieces. Place the remaining pieces in the basket in the center of the game board.
2. The oldest player goes first. The first player rolls the die and moves that number of spaces on the board. Players may move their playing pieces in either direction along the apple path.
3. If a player lands on a number apple, he or she may take that number of apples from the apple basket and place them on his or her tree. If a player lands on a worm, he or she must take two apples off his or her tree and place them back in the apple basket.
4. The first player to fill up his or her apple tree wins the game.

© 1996 Troll Associates/ Troll Early Learning Activities

Folktales and Legends

Johnny Appleseed File-Folder Game

© 1996 Troll Associates/ Troll Early Learning Activities

Folktales and Legends

Johnny Appleseed File-Folder Game

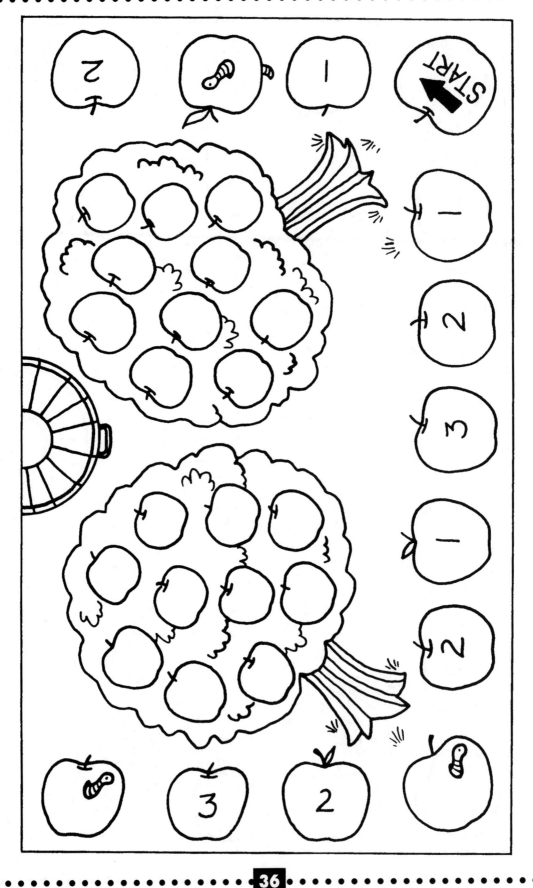

© 1996 Troll Associates/ Troll Early Learning Activities

Johnny Appleseed File-Folder Game

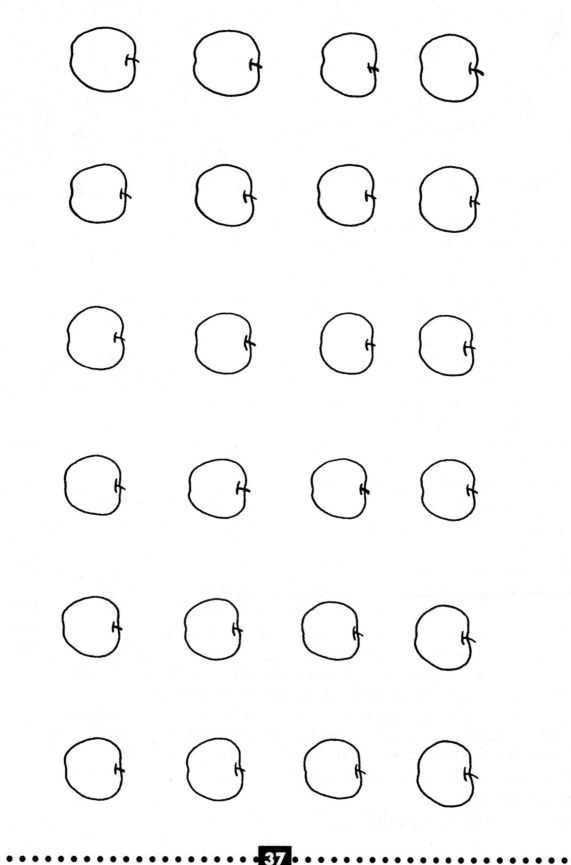

© 1996 Troll Associates/ Troll Early Learning Activities

Little Red Riding Hood

Once upon a time, there lived a charming little girl who was loved by everyone who knew her. Her grandmother loved her most of all, and among the many things she gave her granddaughter was a beautiful red cape. The little girl wore the cape day in and day out, and thus she became known as Little Red Riding Hood.

One day, Little Red Riding Hood's mother asked her to take a basket of food to her grandmother, who was not feeling well. Little Red Riding Hood agreed immediately, because she loved to visit her grandmother.

"But you must promise me that you will go directly to Grandmother's house," said Little Red Riding Hood's mother. "You must not stop to talk to strangers along the way."

Little Red Riding Hood promised her mother, and then she set out on the long journey to her grandmother's house, which was on the other side of the woods. Before too long, though, she came across a big wolf.

"Hello," said the wolf.

"Hello," said Little Red Riding Hood.

"Where are you headed on this fine day?" asked the wolf, smacking his lips hungrily.

"I am going to visit my grandmother," said Little Red Riding Hood. "She is ill, and I am bringing her some food."

"Where does your grandmother live?" asked wolf.

Little Red Riding Hood paused a moment. She remembered her mother telling her not to speak to strangers, but she did not want to be rude to the wolf.

"She lives on the other side of the woods," replied Little Red Riding Hood.

The wolf said to himself, "This little girl would make a delicious meal, but perhaps I can catch both her and her grandmother." Then he said to Little Red Riding Hood, "Well, you'd best be on your way. You mustn't keep your grandmother waiting."

The wolf took off as fast as he could and raced to the grandmother's house. Little Red Riding Hood continued along the path, stopping here and there to pick some flowers for her grandmother. Soon she came across a hunter who was a friend of her grandmother's.

"Hello, Little Red Riding Hood," said the hunter.

"Hello," said Little Red Riding Hood.

"Where are you headed?" asked the hunter.

© 1996 Troll Associates/ Troll Early Learning Activities

Little Red Riding Hood

"I am off to see my grandmother," said Little Red Riding Hood. "She is ill, and I am bringing her food."

"Then I won't keep you," said the hunter. "Please send her my best wishes."

Little Red Riding Hood agreed, and they said their good-byes.

Meanwhile, the wolf had arrived at the grandmother's house. He knocked on the door.

"Who is there?" called the grandmother.

"It is only I, your granddaughter," replied the wolf in a high voice.

"Come in," said the grandmother.

The wolf went into the house and gobbled up the grandmother right away. Then he put on a robe and a cap that was hanging nearby and jumped into her bed.

After a while, Little Red Riding Hood knocked on the door.

"Who is it?" called the wolf.

"It is I, Little Red Riding Hood," the girl answered.

"Come in," said the wolf.

Little Red Riding Hood went into the house and stood next to her grandmother's bed. "Why, Grandmother!" she said. "What big ears you have!"

"The better to hear you with, my dear," said the wolf.

"And what big eyes you have," Little Red Riding Hood said.

"The better to see you with, my dear," said the wolf.

"And, Grandmother, what big teeth you have," said Little Red Riding Hood.

"The better to eat you with, my dear!" roared the wolf. He leapt out of the bed toward Little Red Riding Hood.

Just at that moment, the hunter came through the door. He had decided to stop by to see if the grandmother needed any help. The hunter took out his knife and cut the wolf's throat. Then he quickly slit open the wolf's belly, and out popped the grandmother.

Little Red Riding Hood was so happy to see her grandmother! They both thanked the hunter. The hunter took the wolf's skin for himself, and then went on his way.

And Little Red Riding Hood made another promise, to herself—that she would always do what her mother told her.

© 1996 Troll Associates/ Troll Early Learning Activities

Little Red Riding Hood Flannel Board

Reproduce the patterns on this page and pages 41–42. Color the figures and food basket, mount them on oak-tag, and cut them out. Glue small pieces of flannel or sandpaper to the backs of the shapes. Move the pieces around a flannel board as you read the story "Little Red Riding Hood."

© 1996 Troll Associates/ Troll Early Learning Activities

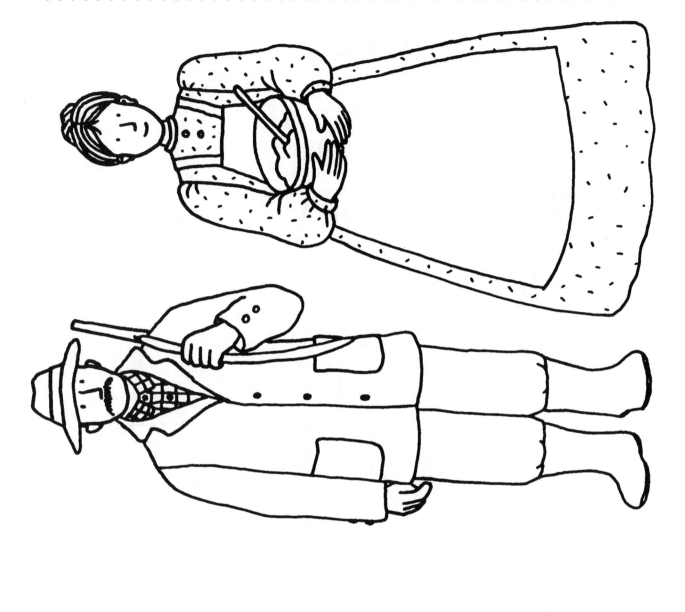

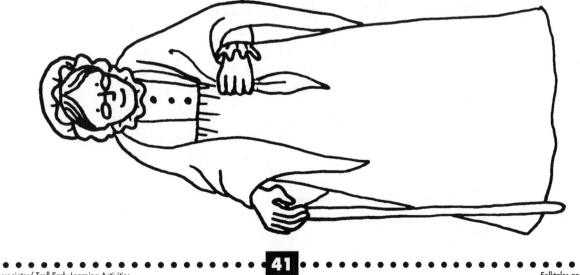

© 1996 Troll Associates/ Troll Early Learning Activities

Folktales and Legends

Little Red Riding Hood Flannel Board

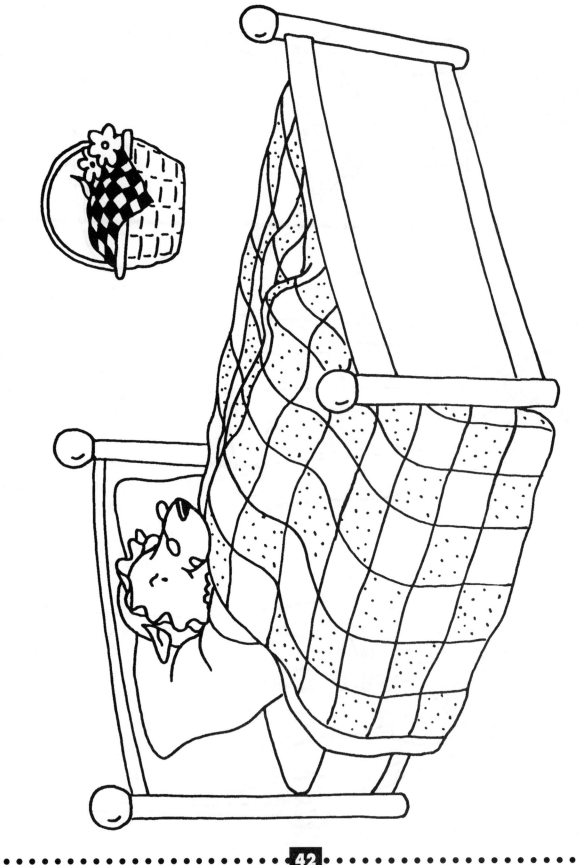

© 1996 Troll Associates/ Troll Early Learning Activities

Name _____

Through the Woods

Help Little Red Riding Hood find the way through the woods to her grandmother's house. Watch out for the wolf!

© 1996 Troll Associates/ Troll Early Learning Activities

Little Red Adjectives

Adjectives are words that describe. *Little* and *red* are both adjectives.

Read each of the sentences below. Underline the adjectives.

1. She has a red cape.

2. What big eyes you have!

3. Grandmother lives in an old house.

4. She walked in the dark woods.

5. The hungry wolf ate the grandmother.

6. The man is a good hunter.

7. The scared girl ran away.

8. She picked some pretty flowers.

9. The grateful grandmother hugged the girl.

10. The story had a happy ending.

© 1996 Troll Associates/ Troll Early Learning Activities

Folktales and Legends

Wolf Paper-Bag Costume

Materials:

- crayons or markers
- glue
- oaktag
- scissors
- hole puncher
- 18" lengths of yarn
- large brown paper grocery bags
- paints and paintbrushes

Directions:

1. Reproduce the wolf mask on page 46 once for each student. Have students color the masks, mount them on oaktag, and cut them out.

2. Help students cut out the eye-holes for the masks.

3. Punch a hole at the left and right sides of each mask, as indicated.

4. Tie an 18" length of yarn through each hole.

5. Distribute a large brown paper grocery bag to each student. Show each student how to cut a hole through the bottom of the bag large enough for his or her head to fit through.

6. Cut armholes and slits up the sides of the paper bags.

7. Have each student paint a wolf body on his or her bag.

8. When dry, let students wear their wolf costumes. Tie the mask to fit around each child's head.

9. Ask volunteers to come up to the front of the class and tell the wolf's side of the story. Encourage students to be creative with their "fractured" fairy tales.

© 1996 Troll Associates/ Troll Early Learning Activities

Folktales and Legends

Wolf Mask

© 1996 Troll Associates/ Troll Early Learning Activities

Folktales and Legends

Paul Bunyan and His Blue Ox

Paul Bunyan was the biggest and best lumberjack who ever lived. He was born in the state of Maine many years ago. When he was born, he weighed 86 pounds!

Paul's appetite matched his size. One day, he ate 74 buckets of oatmeal and drank 14 gallons of milk—and that was just for breakfast!

Paul grew so quickly that his mother had to make him a new set of clothes every week. And legend has it that Paul did not wear shoes until he was fully grown. Before that he simply wore sheets for socks, and barrels for shoes.

When he was still very young, Paul left his parents' farm to seek his fortune. Since he loved the outdoors, Paul decided to become a logger. He took a job at the first logging camp he visited.

One of Paul's favorite chores was that of daybreaker. Paul would head up to the mountains with a big ax to break day and start the morning.

Of course, Paul's ax was the biggest of all. The handle was made of a whole hickory tree, and the blade was the size of a barn door.

Paul quickly became known as the best logger in camp. But one day, he decided to leave the camp and move on to new adventures.

When Paul started out, the Winter of the Blue Snow began. Blue snow fell day after day. One day, Paul tripped over something. Suddenly, he saw a most unusual sight. Sticking out of a snowdrift were two huge, hairy ears!

Naturally, Paul was very curious. He pulled on the ears as hard as he could. And what should come out but a baby blue ox!

This baby was the largest animal Paul had ever seen. His arms shook when he lifted it. Paul rushed home with the baby ox and covered it with blankets. Soon the ox stood up and licked Paul's hand.

"Babe, we'll be great friends!" Paul said happily.

Before long Paul and Babe were working side by side. Paul chopped down the trees. Babe hauled them wherever they needed to go.

Babe grew and grew. Although there were no scales around to weigh the ox, Paul measured the distance between Babe's eyes. It came to 42 ax handles, give or take a handle.

© 1996 Troll Associates/ Troll Early Learning Activities

Paul Bunyan and His Blue Ox

After a time, Paul decided to start his own logging camp. He wanted to make it the biggest logging camp ever. Paul knew he would need plenty of water for such a huge camp. That's when he dug the Great Lakes.

The camp was so large that the workers needed compasses and maps to get around. Many workers got lost. A few were never found.

The cookhouse alone covered 4 square miles. Paul's favorite meal was pancakes. A pipeline was built to bring the syrup right to his table.

Word about Paul's strength spread around the country. Soon he was asked to help out in other places. Once, Paul dug a canal in the middle of the country. While he was digging, he threw dirt to his right and to his left. One pile of dirt became the Rocky Mountains. The other became the Appalachian Mountains. When Babe kicked over a bucket of water to fill it, he made the Mississippi River.

One time Babe was called upon to straighten a crooked road. Paul hitched Babe up to the end of the road. The big ox pulled and pulled. Soon there was a loud CRACK! When things got quiet, the road was perfectly straight.

No one knows where Paul Bunyan is today. One day, he and Babe just headed into the woods and were never heard from again. But if you're ever walking in the forest and hear the cry of "Timber!," don't be surprised if you see a great man and his big, blue ox just around the bend.

Discussion Questions:

1. How do you think Paul's parents felt when he was born?

2. What made Paul such a great logger?

3. Where do you think Babe came from?

4. Why were Paul and Babe such good friends?

5. A tall tale is an unusual story that has been exaggerated as it is retold over the years. What parts of the story of Paul Bunyan do you think have been exaggerated?

6. If you could ask Paul Bunyan to do one great task, what would it be?

© 1996 Troll Associates/ Troll Early Learning Activities

Folktales and Legends

Paul Bunyan and Babe Stick Puppets

Materials:

- crayons or markers
- scissors
- glue
- 18" x 24" sheets of oaktag
- construction paper
- clean junk
- craft sticks

Directions:

1. Reproduce the Paul Bunyan and Babe figures on pages 50-51 once for each student. Have students color the figures, mount them on oaktag, and cut them out.

2. Show students how to glue a craft stick to the bottom of each figure to make a stick puppet.

3. Encourage each student to think of a new adventure for Paul Bunyan and Babe. Have students write down their stories, and then review them together. Tell students that they will be presenting their stories, using their stick puppets, to the rest of the class.

4. Distribute an 18" x 24" piece of oaktag to each student. Ask each student to use the oaktag to make a backdrop for his or her story. Students may fold in each side approximately 8" from the edge so that the backdrop will stand on its own. Students may also wish to make other stick puppets or props using construction paper, clean junk, or other materials.

5. Push two square or rectangular tables long sides together and toward the audience. Cover the front table with a tablecloth that hangs down to the floor.

6. Place a student's backdrop on the back table, facing the audience.

7. Show students how to crawl under the table and then poke the stick puppets up through the space between the two tables. Adjust the backdrop as necessary.

8. Have each student perform his or her story using the stick puppets. If desired, videotape the different adventures. Students may take turns bringing the tape home to share with their families.

© 1996 Troll Associates/ Troll Early Learning Activities   Folktales and Legends

Paul Bunyan and Babe Stick Puppets

© 1996 Troll Associates/ Troll Early Learning Activities

Folktales and Legends

© 1996 Troll Associates/ Troll Early Learning Activities

Where in the World?

After hearing the story of Paul Bunyan answer the following questions. Use an encyclopedia or an atlas if you need help.

1. What state and country share a border with Maine? _____

_____

_____

2. How long is the Mississippi River? In what state does it begin?

_____

_____

3. Through how many states do the Rocky Mountains run? What states are they? _____

_____

_____

4. Through how many states do the Appalachian Mountains run? What states are they? _____

_____

_____

5. Name the Great Lakes. _____

_____

_____

© 1996 Troll Associates/ Troll Early Learning Activities

Missing Words

Fill in the missing word in each of the sentences below.

1. Paul Bunyan weighed 86 pounds when he was __ __ __ (○) .

2. He worked at a logging (○)(○) __ __ .

3. Paul used his ax to __ __ __ __ (○) day.

4. His ax handle was the (○) __ __ __ of a hickory tree.

5. Paul found Babe during the __ __ __ __ (○) __ of the Blue Snow.

6. A (○) __ __ __ __ __ __ __ brought syrup to Paul's table.

7. Babe straightened a crooked __ __ (○) __ .

Write each of the circled letters. Then unscramble the letters to see the name of Paul's favorite food. __ __ __ __ __ __ __ __

© 1996 Troll Associates/ Troll Early Learning Activities

Folktales and Legends

The Sorcerer's Apprentice Rebus Story

Once upon a time, there lived a [sorcerer] who needed to find a helper

for his workshop. The man set off from the [house] where he lived, and

soon he came across a [boy] walking down the [road].

"Hello, there," said the [sorcerer]. "I am looking for an apprentice to help me

in my workshop. Do you know how to read and write?"

"Oh, yes, sir!" said the [boy].

"That's too bad," said the [sorcerer]. "I am looking for someone who does not

know how to read and write."

"I'm sorry, sir," said the [boy], who desperately wanted a job. "I meant to

say that I can't read or write a single word."

And so it came to pass that the [boy] went to live in the [house] with the [sorcerer]

and work as his apprentice. Of course, the [boy] did know how to read and write,

but he did not let on that he had lied.

The man's workshop was a dark and dreary place. The room was filled

with musty old [books], [jars] filled with disgusting-looking things,

and [pots] bubbling over. The [boy] knew immediately that the [sorcerer]

was some kind of witch or sorcerer. He decided to keep quiet and try to learn

everything he could from the sorcerer.

The [boy] worked day and [night] for the [sorcerer]. He collected

strange herbs from the [garden], stirred the brews in the [pots],

and carried down the large, dusty [books] from the high [shelf].

© 1996 Troll Associates/ Troll Early Learning Activities   *Folktales and Legends*

The Sorcerer's Apprentice Rebus Story

After a time, the boy's curiosity started to grow and grow. One day, the 😊 waited until the 😠 went outside to the 🌲🌲, and then he opened one of the old 📖📖. Inside he found pages and pages of evil spells and wicked potions.

"The 😠 is a sorcerer!" gasped the 😊. "And he is an evil sorcerer!" The 😊 read through the pages as quickly as he could. He decided that he would read the 📘📗 as often as he could, and one day become a good 🧙.

The 😊 put the 📕 back on the 📚 before the 😠 was due back. Each day when the 😠 went out to gather the things he needed for his potions, and each 🌙 as the sorcerer soundly 😴💤, the 😊 studied the spells. Then, one day, when the 😠 came back unexpectedly early from his journey, he caught the 😊 casting a spell on the 🐕.

"You lied to me!" roared the 😠, lunging toward the 😊. But the 😊 immediately turned himself into a 🐦 and flew around the room. The 😠, not to be topped, turned himself into a huge 🐈 with powerful claws. The 🐦 landed on a 🪑 and said another spell, turning himself into a 🐻. The 😠, trying to protect himself, turned himself into a 🐟 and jumped into the 🌊 outside the workshop. But the 🐻 jumped in after the 🐟, and gobbled it up.

The 🐻 then changed himself back into a 😊. And from that day forward, only good spells and helpful potions came from the little workshop.

© 1996 Troll Associates/ Troll Early Learning Activities *Folktales and Legends*

The Sorcerer's Apprentice Paper-Bag Puppets

Materials:

- crayons or markers
- scissors
- brown paper lunch bags
- glue
- large paper grocery bag

Directions:

1. Reproduce the patterns on pages 57-59 once. Color the figures and cut them out.

2. Turn a paper lunch bag upside down. Glue the head of any figure except the fish to the bottom of the lunch bag, as shown.

3. Glue the body to the side of the lunch bag, as shown. Repeat for all the figures except the fish.

4. Glue the fish horizontally on a bag, as shown.

5. Use the puppets as story aids when reading "The Sorcerer's Apprentice." Show students how to place their hands inside the puppets and move the bottom flap to indicate when a character is talking or moving.

6. Distribute the rebus story "The Sorcerer's Apprentice" to the class. Place the puppets in a large paper grocery bag in the reading or dramatic play center for students to use to act out the story on their own. If desired, allow students to make other puppets and encourage them to create new story lines of their own.

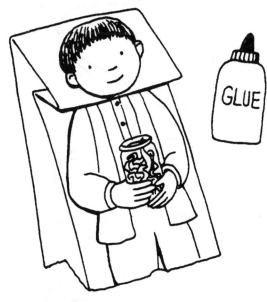

© 1996 Troll Associates/ Troll Early Learning Activities

Folktales and Legends

The Sorcerer's Apprentice Paper-Bag Puppets

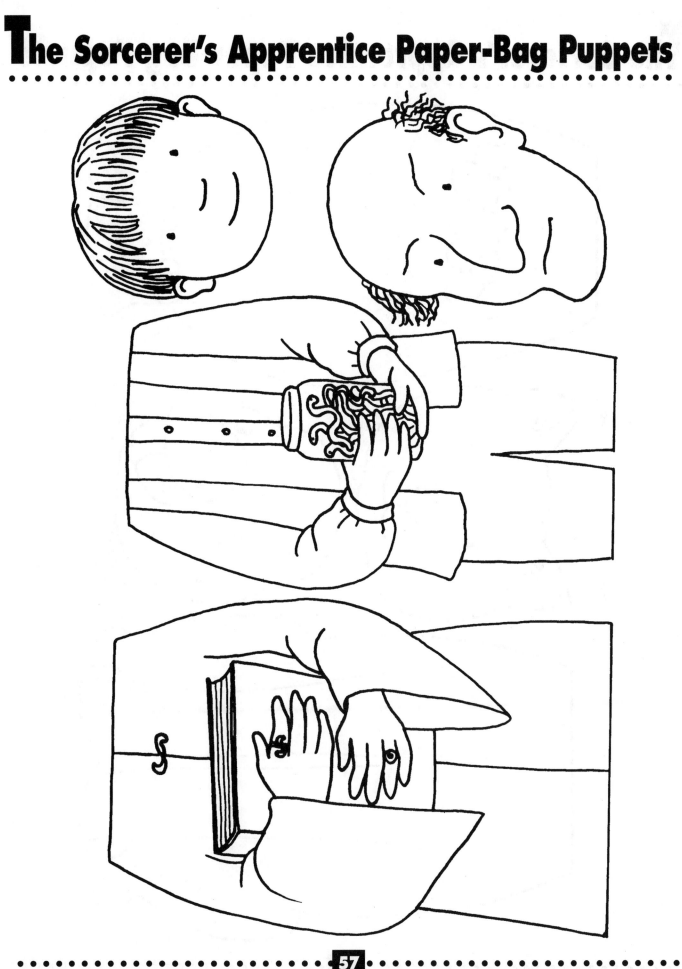

© 1996 Troll Associates/ Troll Early Learning Activities

Folktales and Legends

© 1996 Troll Associates/ Troll Early Learning Activities

Folktales and Legends

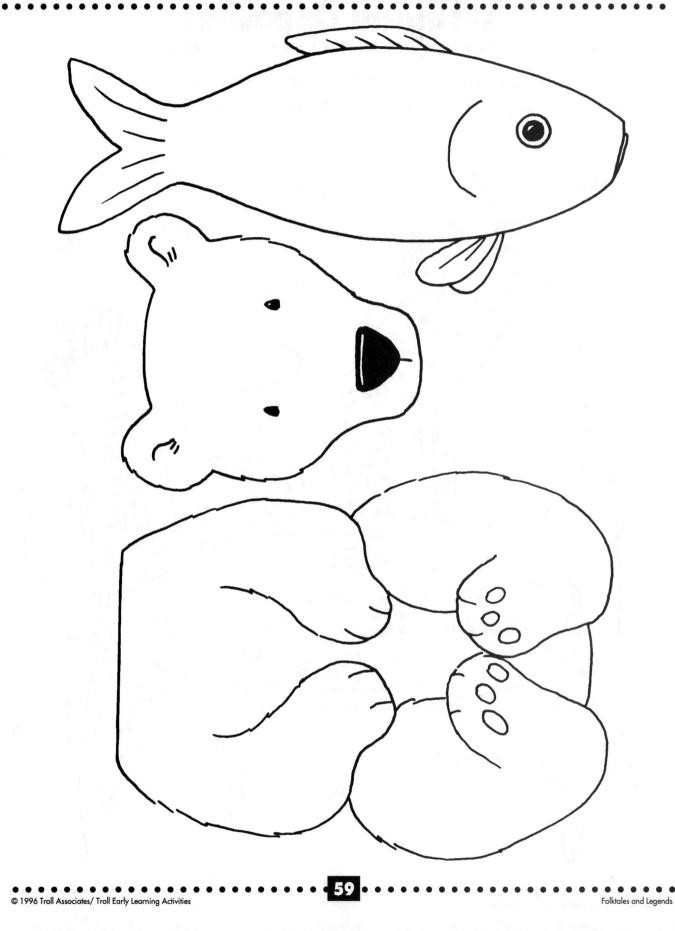

© 1996 Troll Associates/ Troll Early Learning Activities

Folktales and Legends

Name_____

Magical Opposites

The sorcerer is brewing up a pot of mean-spirited words. To help the boy foil the sorcerer's plans, draw lines to connect each of the sorcerer's words to its opposite.

beautiful

friend

smile

lucky

nice

fix

best

evil   mean

ugly   worst   hurt

unfortunate   break   frown

cloudy   enemy

good

help

sunny

© 1996 Troll Associates/ Troll Early Learning Activities   Folktales and Legends

Name _____

First Things First

Look at each of the pictures below illustrating the story "The Sorcerer's Apprentice." On the line next to each picture, write 1 for the scene that happens first, 2 for the scene that happens second, and so on.

Next, cut the pictures apart along the dotted lines. Glue them to another piece of paper in the correct order.

© 1996 Troll Associates/ Troll Early Learning Activities

Folktales and Legends

Award

Class Storyteller

_____

presented by _____

on _____

Short Stories

© 1996 Troll Associates/ Troll Early Learning Activities

Folktales and Legends

Class Playwright

presented to:

by _____

on _____

© 1996 Troll Associates/ Troll Early Learning Activities

UNIVERSITY OF RHODE ISLAND
3 1222 01044 5719

NO LONGER THE PROPER
OF THE
UNIVERSITY OF R.I. LIBRARY

Answers

page 12

page 22

Answers will vary.

page 23

Answers will vary.

page 24

8 + 1 = red; 12 - 2 = orange; 4 + 3 = blue; 20 - 10 = orange;
6 + 3 = red; 5 + 3 = yellow; 2 + 7 = red; 10 - 2 = yellow;
5 + 4 = red; 15 - 8 = blue; 20 - 10 = orange; 14 - 5 = red;
7 + 3 = orange; 4 + 4 = yellow; 2 + 5 = blue; 12 - 3 = red;
6 + 2 = yellow; 10 - 3 = blue; 5 + 5 = orange;
9 - 1 = yellow; 11 - 2 = red

page 25

Answers will vary.

page 29

1. troll
2. ghost
3. ghoul
4. monster
5. vampire
6. werewolf
7. goblin
8. witch
9. gremlin
10. phantom
11. giant
12. warlock

page 43

page 44

1. She has a red cape.
2. What big eyes you have!
3. Grandmother lives in an old house.
4. She walked in the dark woods.
5. The hungry wolf ate the grandmother.
6. The man is a good hunter.
7. The scared girl ran away.
8. She picked some pretty flowers.
9. The grateful grandmother hugged the girl.
10. The story had a happy ending.

page 52

1. New Hampshire and Canada
2. 2,348 miles (3,779 km); Minnesota
3. six; Montana, Idaho, Wyoming, Utah, Colorado, New Mexico
4. 12: Maine, New Hampshire, Vermont, New York, New Jersey, Pennsylvania, Maryland, West Virginia, North Carolina, Georgia, Tennessee, Kentucky
5. Superior, Huron, Michigan, Erie, and Ontario

page 53

1. born
2. camp
3. break
4. size
5. winter
6. pipeline
7. road

PANCAKES

page 60

evil—good; mean—nice; ugly—beautiful; worst—best; hurt—help; unfortunate—lucky; break—fix; frown—smile; cloudy—sunny; enemy—friend

page 61

© 1996 Troll Associates/ Troll Early Learning Activities

Folktales and Legends